_____

"You've made this day a special day, by just your being you. There's no person in the whole world like you, and I like you just the way you are."

- Fred Rogers

Written and Illustrated by Ariane O'Pry Trammell

Book Design by Ariane O'Pry Trammell

Edited by Monica Robertson

ISBN: 978-0-9863485-9-4

This book is self-published by

Ariane O'Pry Trammell

"When I Grow Up… I Want to Be Me!"

When I Grow Up...

I Want to Be Me!

Written & Illustrated by
Ariane O'Pry Trammell

Often, I imagine

what I might become

someday...

As I'm learning and I'm growing,

as I'm

finding

my own way.

Will I be a firefighter
braving flames

and saving

lives?

Will I serve as military...
defending our freedom,
protecting our rights?

Will **I** be a missionary,
reaching out to share **Go**d's word?

Will I be a farmer
growing crops
to feed the world?

Perhaps I'll be a doctor, helping people to feel better.

Or a postal worker delivering letters, no matter the weather.

Will I be a teacher
giving children education?

KINDNESS

COURAGE

FRIENDSHIP

HARD WORK

Kellan
Gavin
Destyn
Wyatt ✓
Gunner
Kinsley
Hudson ✓
Thomas ✓✓

Mr. Johnny's Classroo

1×1=
1×2=
x3=
1=

I might even be the President...
the leader of our nation!

The most important thing of all
is that I will remember...

GOd has a plan
meant just for me,
and I'm
a Special treasure.

We come in many colors,

shapes and sizes

of all sorts.

Some have
extraordinary
minds,

and some have
different
parts.

My life is precious...
priceless from the moment I was formed.
Our Holy Father knew and loved me

before I was born.

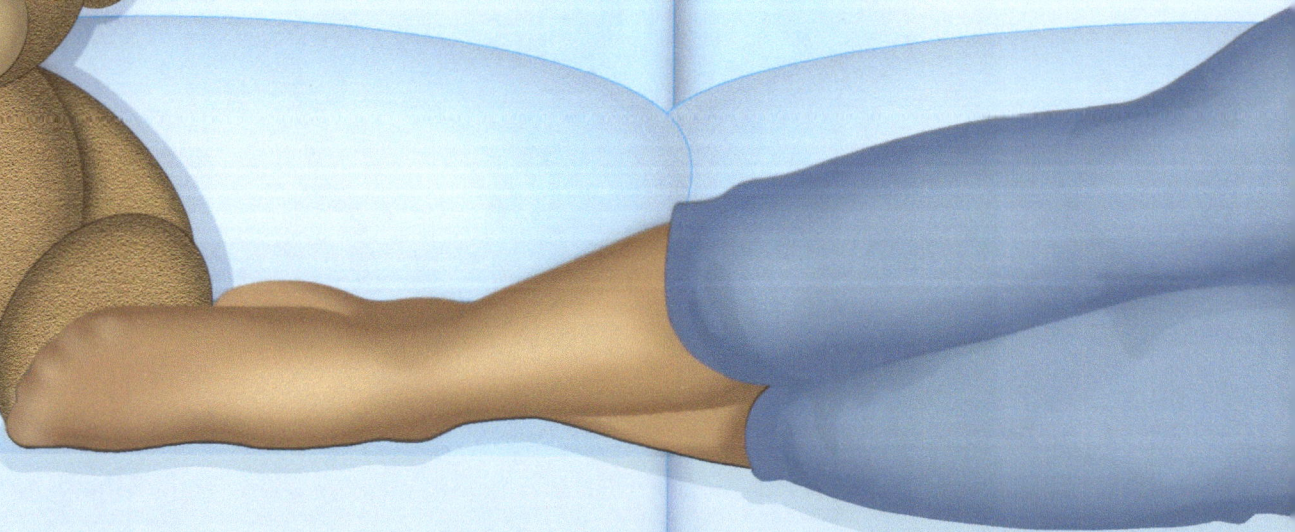

We're all sculpted by His hands...
unique in every way,

blessed with gifts and talents
we'll discover every day.

I may not yet be certain
of the path that I will take,
but I'm a child of God;
and I will always walk by faith.

I'll listen to His still, small voice

and let Him take the lead.

No matter what I might grow up to be...

I'll be proud to be

ME!

DEDICATION

This book is dedicated in honor and memory of Mr. Fred Rogers. He devoted his inspiring life and career to assuring each and every child that they were special and exceptional by simply being themselves. He taught them that they were precious and deserving of love. In the book of Leviticus we're told to love our neighbor as ourselves. In achieving this, we should first learn to fully embrace and appreciate who we're created to be. I feel that God's plan for my life is to share these teachings through my books. I grew up watching *Mr. Rogers Neighborhood* and I truly believe that his program left a life-long impression upon me. His mission helped to sculpt and refine me into the ambitious Christian woman that I am today. Should I achieve even a fraction of Fred's positive impact on the precious little minds of America, I will have done a beautiful service to both my country and my God. Thank you so much, Mr. Rogers, for growing up to be you.

"You've made this day a special day, by just your being you. There's no person in the whole world like you, and I like you just the way you are."

- Fred Rogers

ABOUT THE AUTHOR/ILLUSTRATOR

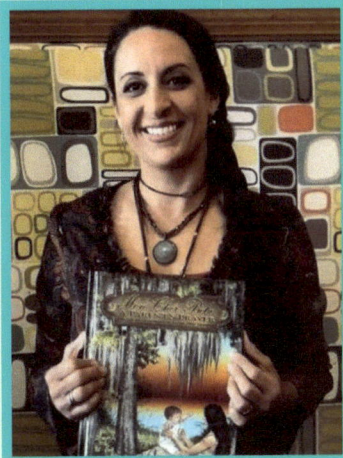

Ariane O'Pry Trammell is an artist and children's book author/illustrator from the small town of Ponchatoula, Louisiana. After having illustrated numerous publications for other authors and guiding them through the process of self-publishing, she was encouraged to write a children's book of her own. Her first, "*Where the Grass is Always Greener*" was released in 2013.

As the mother of two young sons, Kellan and Gavin, Ariane is constantly inspired to create. Often featured in her illustrations, her children are even depicted as the main characters, Boudin and T-boy, in her very successful Cajun series. She launched the first book of that series, "*Run! Boudin, Run!*" in 2016. "*Cicada's Song*" was soon to follow in 2017. "*Couillon the Crawfish*" made his debut in 2018. In 2019 Ariane released another stand-alone title, "*Mon Cher Bebe, 'A Parent's Prayer'.*"

She finds herself immensely blessed in having a career that is truly her passion and God-given gift. Ariane is also a member of the historic French Market in New Orleans where she regularly sells her books. She often visits schools and libraries to share her stories.

Ariane is excited to continue on her path in children's literature by introducing, "*When I Grow Up... I Want to Be Me!*" She hopes to inspire, encourage and instill a love of reading ans art in every child.

Kellan and Gavin Trammell

A NOTE TO MY PRECIOUS LITTLE READERS

This book is very close to my heart. I'd been kicking around the idea of writing a book about self-esteem and uniqueness, but it didn't seem to come easily. I had been so frustrated, as I prayed for the right words to come. I prepared myself. I was fully aware, alert and listening. I would receive my book in His time, and then follow His instruction. I was finally inspired to write it as I was sitting in church one morning. The speaker said, "If you don't grow up to be you, then who will?" The instant I heard those words it was as if God had dropped that book right into my head. I started writing as it was pouring out of me faster than my pencil could be pushed. My original manuscript was on paper in no more than 10 minutes.

I was so excited about my new mission. I have faith that if God's hand is in it, and it's His will for me to take on a project, it simply cannot fail. If I keep my focus on Him and work hard, He'll open the doors and light my path. In all of my achievements, I glorify God and thank Him for the beautiful gifts I've been blessed with. I utilize them with love, to do good things for others. I use them for service.

I didn't always feel so positive, nor did I imagine that I might be called upon to share my gifts. Growing up, I was a fairly awkward child. I struggled with my self-esteem. I was horribly bullied in elementary school. My gift... my expression... my escape was always art. I would never tire of drawing or striving to become better, and it was something that I was very good at.

Being gifted in the arts often goes hand-in-hand with having ADD and/or OCD. I have been diagnosed with both. While many struggles have been prompted by these "disorders," I can't help but feel grateful for them. Had I not been gifted a brain with ADD, I might not be a dreamer. I might not possess the vision and creativity that I do. Had I not been gifted a brain with OCD, I might lack the obsessive attention to detail that's employed in my work. I might not possess the discipline and determination to be self-taught in my craft. Though I haven't always been thankful for these traits, I love and embrace them now.

I was quite a little space cadet; always floating around in my own little world of wonder, or doodling in my notebook when I should have been more focused in class. My older son, Kellan, faces many of the same challenges. It hurts my heart deeply when he struggles. I can closely relate to his pain and frustration. I'm immensely grateful that he has the opportunity to receive resource accommodations at school. This help was not available to me throughout my elementary years.

When you're a child in school, there is so much importance centered upon academic strengths. If you do your very best, but still miss the mark, it can be very discouraging. You may begin to feel like the only thing that seems to matter is something you're no good at. You may stress about finding your purpose in life or wonder how you'll ever have a career doing something that you love. While it is very important that we are educated and strive for knowledge in school, don't neglect or lose sight of your God-given talents. Pursue growth unceasingly and continue to develop them.

Some of us don't feel that we fit in. We might feel self-conscious because we're different. Some experience sadness and loneliness because of their uniqueness. Perhaps you have strengths that many people lack. Maybe you excel in art the way I do. You may have a passion for music. You might be great at making friends laugh. Those gifts may not seem so significant to you now, but don't worry. Don't doubt yourself. God has equipped you with ALL that you need in order to blossom, thrive, and to grow into that amazing individual you're becoming every day. We're ALL created by our God with SO much love and care . He makes NO mistakes. Every "imperfection" is crafted for a divine destiny.

I hope that you'll always find beauty, happiness and purpose in yourself; in being just the way you are. I also hope that others around you will only encourage and uplift you. I pray that you'll never have to suffer the pain of being bullied and mistreated by your peers. Be true you yourself, little one. Embrace who you are. Remain humble in your success and remember there is always room to grow. Build a close, meaningful relationship with God. Pray for guidance and courage often.

I'm grateful for your support and interest in my work. I hope that you'll cherish your book and it's message. Thank you for appreciating the "ME" that I've become!

-Ariane O'Pry Trammell

Like & Follow Ariane on Facebook for updates on
future releases and scheduled signing events!
Facebook.com/arianetrammellbooks

For more information about Ariane and her arts, visit her website!
Arianesart.com

To schedule a signing event or book presentation with Ariane, contact her directly!
artbyariane@hotmail.com
(985)634-4721

To order books online, find them now on Amazon.com!
(Books ordered through Amazon will not be signed or personalized and do not include the
bonus video link. Contact Ariane directly to order signed/personalized copies.)

Retail customers can order books wholesale through Ingram!

To view the **BONUS VIDEO** version of this book online,
copy the following link into the address bar in your browser!

https://_____

www.ingramcontent.com/pod-product-compliance
Lightning Source LLC
Chambersburg PA
CBHW042009090426
42811CB00015B/1591

9 780986 348594